CHRISTIAN McCAFFREY

Sports Superstars

BY THOMAS K. ADAMSON

TORQUE

BELLWETHER MEDIA · MINNEAPOLIS, MN

Torque brims with excitement perfect for thrill-seekers of all kinds. Discover daring survival skills, explore uncharted worlds, and marvel at mighty engines and extreme sports. In *Torque* books, anything can happen. Are you ready?

This edition first published in 2026 by Bellwether Media, Inc.

No part of this publication may be reproduced in whole or in part without written permission of the publisher. For information regarding permission, write to Bellwether Media, Inc., Attention: Permissions Department, 3500 American Blvd W, Suite 150, Bloomington, MN 55431.

Library of Congress Cataloging-in-Publication Data

LC record for Christian McCaffrey available at: https://lccn.loc.gov/2025013767

Text copyright © 2026 by Bellwether Media, Inc. TORQUE and associated logos are trademarks and/or registered trademarks of Bellwether Media, Inc. Bellwether Media is a division of FlutterBee Education Group.

Editor: Kieran Downs   Designer: Gabriel Hilger

Printed in the United States of America, North Mankato, MN.

TABLE OF CONTENTS

SUPER BOWL BOUND	4
WHO IS CHRISTIAN McCAFFREY?	6
COLLEGE STAR	8
NFL STAR	12
McCAFFREY'S FUTURE	20
GLOSSARY	22
TO LEARN MORE	23
INDEX	24

SUPER BOWL BOUND

The 49ers trail the Lions 14–0 in the 2023 NFC **Championship** Game. Christian McCaffrey takes a handoff. He runs through the other team on his way into the **end zone**. He scores a **touchdown**!

The big score gets the 49ers started on a comeback. They go on to win and advance to the **Super Bowl**!

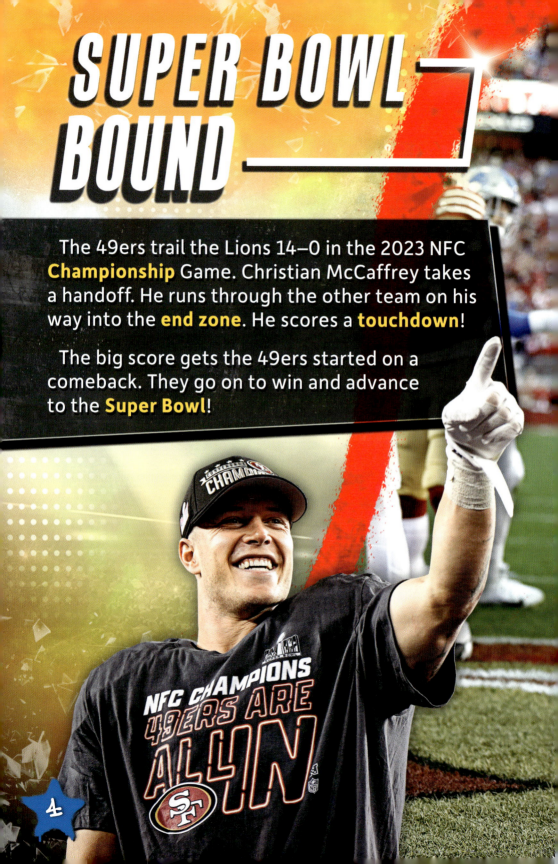

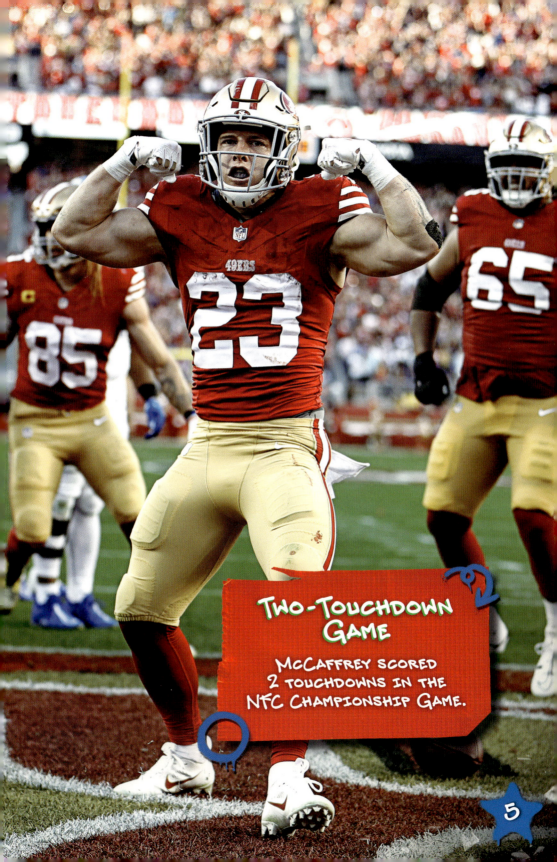

WHO IS CHRISTIAN McCAFFREY?

Christian McCaffrey is a **running back** in the **National Football League** (NFL). He is known for running with toughness. It is hard to tackle him. He is also a threat to catch passes.

CHRISTIAN McCAFFREY

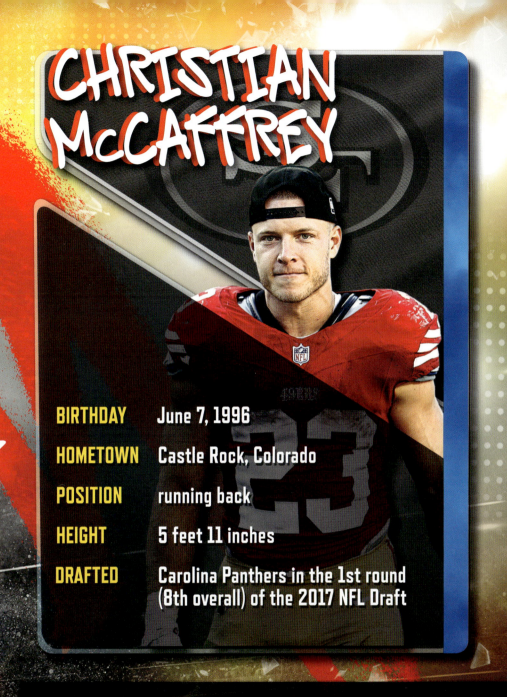

BIRTHDAY	June 7, 1996
HOMETOWN	Castle Rock, Colorado
POSITION	running back
HEIGHT	5 feet 11 inches
DRAFTED	Carolina Panthers in the 1st round (8th overall) of the 2017 NFL Draft

McCaffrey was the 2023 **Offensive** Player of the Year. He helped the San Francisco 49ers reach Super Bowl 58 that season.

COLLEGE STAR

McCaffrey comes from a sports family. His dad played in the NFL for 13 seasons. His older brother, Max, played briefly in the NFL. His younger brother Luke started playing for the Washington Commanders in 2024.

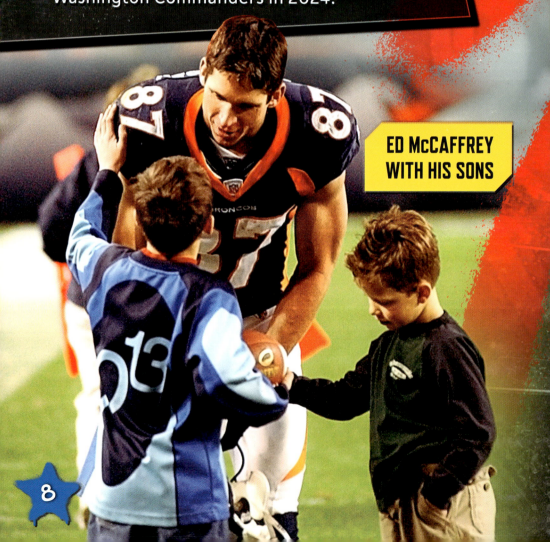

ED McCAFFREY WITH HIS SONS

Fast Runner

McCaffrey was also a sprinter in track and field.

McCaffrey helped his high school team win four Colorado state titles. He won the Gatorade State Player of the Year award in 2013 and 2014.

McCaffrey went to college at Stanford University. In 2015, he broke the college record for most **all-purpose** yards in a season with 3,864 combined yards. He was named the AP College Football Player of the Year. He also helped Stanford win the **Rose Bowl**.

McCaffrey played well in 2016, too. He set a Stanford single-game rushing record with 284 yards.

2016 ROSE BOWL

Rose Bowl Record

In the 2016 Rose Bowl, McCaffrey gained over 100 rushing and receiving yards. He was the first player in the history of the Rose Bowl to do so.

FAVORITES

MOVIE	SNACK	SINGER	HOBBY

Enter the Dragon	Cool Ranch Doritos	Tyler Childers	playing piano

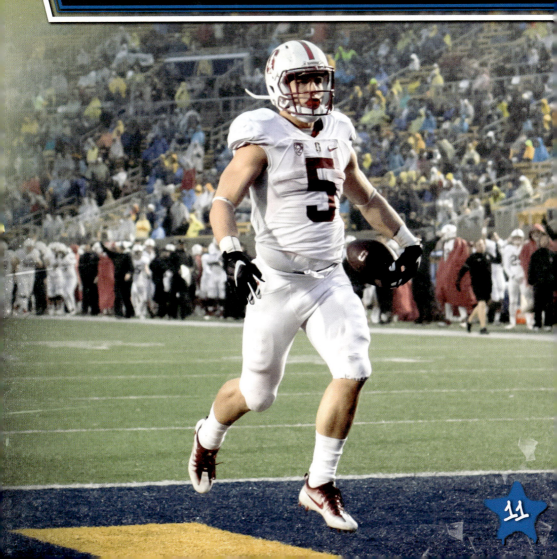

NFL STAR

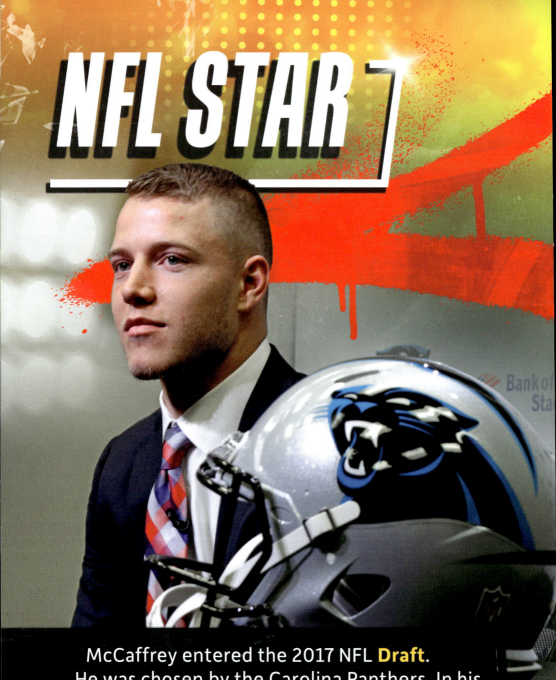

McCaffrey entered the 2017 NFL **Draft**. He was chosen by the Carolina Panthers. In his first year, he helped them reach the **playoffs**.

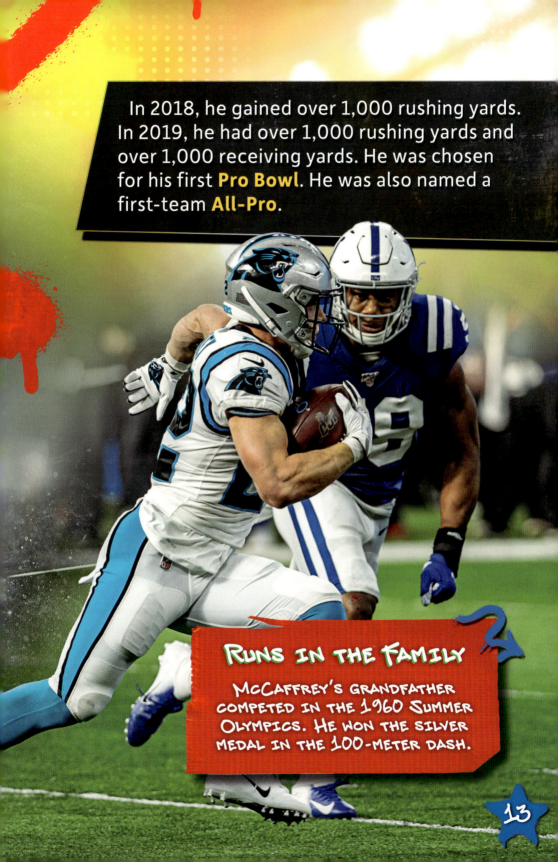

In 2018, he gained over 1,000 rushing yards. In 2019, he had over 1,000 rushing yards and over 1,000 receiving yards. He was chosen for his first **Pro Bowl**. He was also named a first-team **All-Pro**.

Runs in the Family

McCaffrey's grandfather competed in the 1960 Summer Olympics. He won the silver medal in the 100-meter dash.

In 2020, McCaffrey signed a deal with the Panthers. It made him the highest-paid running back in NFL history.

McCaffrey started the 2020 season strong. But he got hurt early in the season. He missed many games. McCaffrey was hurt again during much of the 2021 season.

CHRISTIAN McCAFFREY MAP

- Carolina Panthers, Charlotte, North Carolina — 2017 to 2022
- San Francisco 49ers, Santa Clara, California — 2022 to present

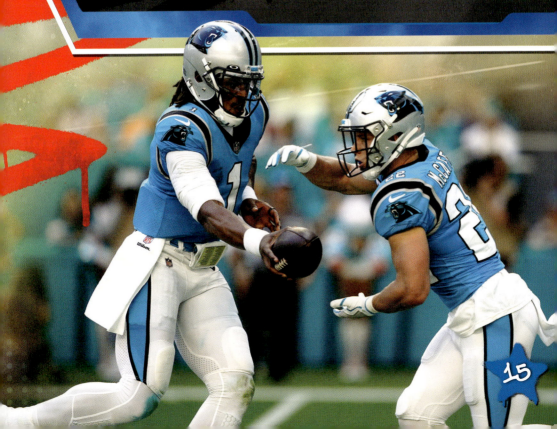

McCaffrey was healthy for the 2022 season. He rushed for 393 yards in six games with the Panthers.

In October, the Panthers traded McCaffrey to the San Francisco 49ers. McCaffrey helped his new team reach the playoffs. But they lost in the NFC Championship Game. McCaffrey was also named to his second Pro Bowl that season.

Record Breaker

McCaffrey reached 3,000 rushing yards and 3,000 receiving yards faster than any player in NFL history. He did it in 57 games.

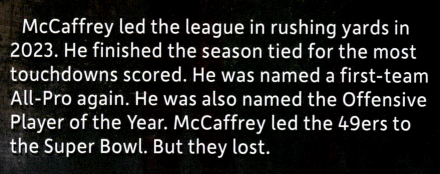

McCaffrey led the league in rushing yards in 2023. He finished the season tied for the most touchdowns scored. He was named a first-team All-Pro again. He was also named the Offensive Player of the Year. McCaffrey led the 49ers to the Super Bowl. But they lost.

In 2024, he was hurt again. He missed many games.

2023 OFFENSIVE PLAYER OF THE YEAR

TIMELINE

— 2016 —
McCaffrey helps Stanford win the Rose Bowl

— 2017 —
McCaffrey is drafted by the Panthers

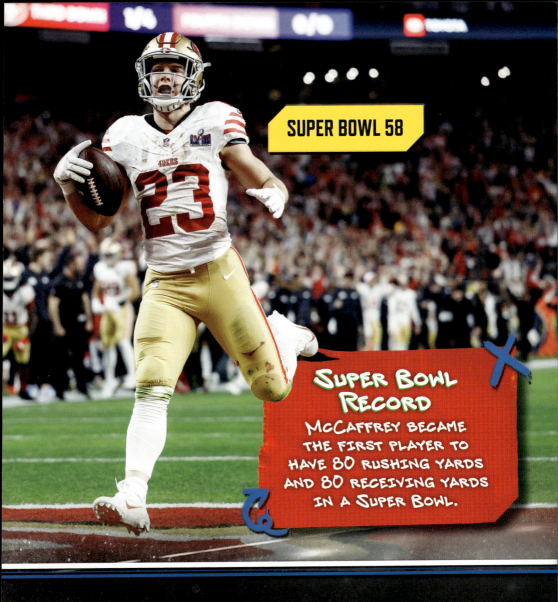

SUPER BOWL 58

Super Bowl Record

McCaffrey became the first player to have 80 rushing yards and 80 receiving yards in a Super Bowl.

— 2019 —
McCaffrey is named a first-team All-Pro

— 2022 —
McCaffrey is traded to the 49ers

— 2024 —
McCaffrey plays in Super Bowl 58

19

McCAFFREY'S FUTURE

McCaffrey started the Christian McCaffrey **Foundation**. This **charity** helps support military members and their families. It also helps support children's hospitals.

McCaffrey signed a new deal with the 49ers in 2024. It keeps him with the team through 2027. He wants to lead the 49ers to another Super Bowl!

GLOSSARY

All-Pro—an honor for football players who are the best at each position during a season

all-purpose—related to the total of a player's rushing and receiving yards

championship—a contest to decide the best team or person

charity—an organization that helps others in need

draft—a process where professional teams choose high school and college athletes to play for them

end zone—the area on either end of a football field

foundation—an organization that helps people and communities

National Football League—a professional football league in the United States; the National Football League is often called the NFL.

offensive—related to players who have the ball and are trying to score

playoffs—games played after the regular season is over; playoff games determine which teams play in the championship game.

Pro Bowl—a game between the best players in the National Football League

Rose Bowl—the oldest and most famous of the college football bowl games; bowl games are college football games played after the regular season is over.

running back—a player on a football team who carries the ball on running plays

Super Bowl—the annual championship game of the National Football League

touchdown—a score that occurs when a team crosses into their opponent's end zone with the football; a touchdown is worth six points.

TO LEARN MORE

AT THE LIBRARY

Lowe, Alexander. *G.O.A.T. Football Running Backs.* Minneapolis, Minn.: Lerner Publications, 2023.

Roggio, Sarah. *Christian McCaffrey vs. LaDainian Tomlinson: Who Would Win?* Minneapolis, Minn.: Lerner Publications, 2025.

Whiting, Jim. *The Story of the San Francisco 49ers.* Mankato, Minn.: Creative Education, 2025.

ON THE WEB

Factsurfer.com gives you a safe, fun way to find more information.

1. Go to www.factsurfer.com

2. Enter "Christian McCaffrey" into the search box and click.

3. Select your book cover to see a list of related content.

INDEX

awards, 7, 9, 10, 18
Carolina Panthers, 12, 14, 16
childhood, 8, 9
Christian McCaffrey Foundation, 20
Colorado, 9
deal, 14, 21
draft, 12
family, 8, 13
favorites, 11
first-team All-Pro, 13, 18
hurt, 14, 18
map, 15
National Football League, 6, 8, 12, 14, 16
NFC Championship Game, 4, 5, 16, 17
playoffs, 12, 16
Pro Bowl, 13, 16
profile, 7
record, 10, 16, 19
Rose Bowl, 10
running back, 6, 14
San Francisco 49ers, 4, 7, 16, 18, 21
sprinter, 9
Stanford University, 10
Super Bowl, 4, 7, 18, 19, 21
timeline, 18–19
touchdown, 4, 5, 18
trophy shelf, 17
yards, 10, 13, 16, 18, 19

The images in this book are reproduced through the courtesy of: Jeff Lewis/ AP Images, front cover; ZUMA Press, Inc./ Alamy Stock Photo, pp. 3, 13; Cooper Neill/ Contributor/ Getty Images, p. 4; Michael Zagaris/ Contributor/ Getty Images, pp. 5, 21; Kevin Sabitus/ Contributor/ Getty Images, p. 6; Michael Owens/ Contributor/ Getty Images, p. 7 (Christian McCaffrey); Cyrus McCrimmon/ Contributor/ Getty Images, p. 8; Hyoung Chang/ Contributor/ Getty Images, p. 9; Sean M. Haffey/ Staff/ Getty Images, p. 10; seeshooteatrepeat, p. 11 (Enter the Dragon); Steve Cukrov, p. 11 (Cool Ranch Doritos); Sipa USA/ Alamy Stock Photo, p. 11 (Tyler Childers); borisblik, p. 11 (playing piano); David Madison/ Contributor/ Getty Images, p. 11 (Christian McCaffrey); Chuck Burton/ AP Images, p. 12; Jeff Roberson/ AP Images, p. 14; Zenstratus, p. 15 (Carolina Panthers stadium); SarahSchmidt, p. 15 (San Francisco 49ers stadium); Lynne Sladky/ AP Images, p. 15 (Christian McCaffrey); Cal Sport Media/ Alamy Stock Photo, pp. 16, 17; Perry Knotts/ AP Images, p. 18 (2023 Offensive Player of the year); Icon Sports Wire/ Contributor/ Getty Images, p. 18 (2016); Carolina Panthers/ Wikipedia, p. 18 (Carolina Panthers logo); Ryan Kang/ Contributor/ Getty Images, p. 19 (Super bowl 58); San Francisco 49ers/ Wikipedia, p. 19 (San Francisco 49ers logo); Ezra Shaw/ Staff/ Getty Images, p. 19 (2024); Andy Cross/ MediaNews Group/ The Denver Post via Getty Images/ Contributor/ Getty Images, p. 20; Lachlan Cunningham/ Contributor/ Getty Images, p. 23.